The *Scottish Baking* Bible

The *Scottish Baking* Bible

Liz Ashworth

Illustrated by Bob Dewar

BIRLINN

First published in Great Britain in 2020 by
Birlinn Ltd
West Newington House
10 Newington Road
Edinburgh
EH9 1QS

www.birlinn.co.uk

ISBN: 978 1 78027 634 2

British Library Cataloguing-in-Publication Data
A catalogue record for this book is available on
request from the British Library

Designed and typeset by Mark Blackadder

Printed and bound in Britain by
Bell & Bain Ltd, Glasgow

Contents

Pastries, Tarts and Traybakes

Cakes and Wee Fancies

Preface

I remember the appetising aromas of fresh baking that greeted my sister Sue and me when we returned from school and opened the kitchen door on the day that our mother 'filled the tins'. She made family favourites like gypsy creams, waffle biscuits, lemon shorties, wee rock cakes and Father's favourite girdle scones. He loved them warm from the girdle smothered with butter and Mum's home-made 'rasser' jam. During my childhood in the early 1950s commercially produced packets of biscuits, tarts and cakes were almost unknown and the serve-yourself supermarket had not yet arrived. It was a normal part of the week for the housewife to have a 'baking day'.

Enterprising local bakers displayed their hand-made biscuits in glass-fronted cabinets with drawers or similar large tins filled with perkins, butter biscuits, rice biscuits, shortbreads and other tempting delicacies. The chosen biscuits were popped into deep paper bags and the corners twisted to keep the contents safe inside as they jiggled in our shopping basket on its travels around the local shops. In my home town of Elgin alone, I can remember at least eight bakers, and each had a speciality. Austin's were famed for their fabulous confectionery, Brumley Brae shortbread and croissant rolls; upstairs from the shop was an Art Deco tea room which is still there today. Morris's made the best meringues; Murray the baker did a dark crusted plain loaf; Duthie's were known for morning rolls and cheese bread, and Smillie's for delicious chocolate hazelnut biscuits.

My mother was a domestic science teacher so I was off to a good start in the kitchen department. My first memory of 'baking' is of standing on a stool while mixing a flour and water paste in a cup which Mum had coloured pink with cochineal. I would have been about three years old – she started me young! I soon progressed to helping measure, mix and make cakes and simple biscuits – not forgetting the all-important bowl scraping! I loved baking and soon was filling the tins to help my mother, who had returned to work. Mummy Clerk next door and Rena Loud, who lived opposite, also encouraged me to cook and bake. Rena gave me my first recipe notebook and I still have it filled with a lifetime of recipes and the memories they evoke.

Not far from Austin's bakery was the Girls' Technical College, now Moray Council offices. In the early 1960s it was a busy place where we learned to cook and to sew. Mrs Barclay taught us the basics of cookery and then a new young teacher introduced us to a different food world. I still have my *Glasgow Cookery Book* filled with notes and recipes from that time. Imagine my good fortune because that young teacher, who has become a good friend and mentor, is the well-known food writer and food historian Catherine Brown.

The seed was well and truly sown back then. Give me a kitchen and the wherewithal to bake and I am content.

Introduction

'If every French woman is born with a wooden spoon in her hand, every Scotswoman is born with a rolling pin under her arm. There may be a divergence of opinion as to her skill in cooking, but it is certain that she has developed a remarkable technique in baking – not only in bannocks, scones and oatcakes, but also in the finer manipulations of wheat – in cakes, pastry and shortbread.'

F. Marian McNeill, *The Scots Kitchen*, 1929

The story of Scotland's baking tradition began with a circle of hot stones round a fire on which the Gaels baked barley and oats into 'hearth cakes', known as bannocks. A bannock is a round flat unleavened cake of grain. The circle of stones named 'greadeal' points to the beginnings of the Scottish baking plate called a 'girdle'. This metal plate has its origins in the Iron Age, as does the large pot which hung over the fire.

The cast-iron girdle was invented in Culross, Fife, the

manufacture of which James VI granted exclusivity in 1599. This lapsed when iron works began mass producing cheaper girdles.

How did it all begin?

For centuries bere, an ancient form of barley, and subsequently oats were mainstays of the Scottish diet. Contrary to popular belief, bere was the staple dating back over 5,000 years to Neolithic times, and a form of the grain still grows on Orkney today. Bere, a nutrient-rich six-row barley, grows quickly in the north's short growing season and cooler climate. This grain fed men and animals alike and place names like Bearsden show its historic importance.

However, bere is difficult to harvest, thresh and store and does not keep as well as oats, which gradually led to its decline in use during the seventeenth century as improved farming methods and more productive varieties of oats were introduced.

Oatmeal stored well: tightly packed into a meal girnel (chest) it would keep over the winter and was readily made into brose, porridge, bannocks or oatcakes. Wheat also grew in areas with a milder climate and better soil, initially as a cash crop sold as grain but rarely ground locally into flour. Taxes and indentures influenced which grains farmers grew, millers milled and, inevitably, what was baked and eaten.

Oats were really one of the first convenience foods, being nutritious, sustaining and easily cooked. A mixture of oatmeal and water made the first oatcakes. Scottish soldiers would each carry a small bag of oatmeal and a metal plate which was heated in the fire to bake a paste of oats and water into an 'oatcake'. Little currency was in circulation so the staples, bere and oats, were a valuable commodity used to pay rent, wages, the minister's stipend, even dowries! Bartering of food was commonplace. Trade in live cattle was a major source of income and thieving was common. One influential Highland laird, Barrisdale, was one of many who protected weaker lairds for a fee, paid in oats, called 'black-meal', which is thought to be the root of the word 'blackmail'.

'The girdle until recent times took the place of the oven, the bannock, the loaf.'
F. Marian McNeill, *The Scots Kitchen*, 1929

The bannocks or 'kaaks' of oatmeal we now know as oatcakes became synonymous with Scotland, which was often referred to as 'the land o' cakes'! Each housewife had her own recipe handed down over generations. Practice taught how the dough should look and feel without weighing ingredients. She used utensils such as a stick or 'spurtle' to stir the dough, a thin notched rolling pin called a 'bannock-stick' to roll out, a long handled 'spathe' like a heart-shaped fish slice to lift the oatcakes on and off the hot girdle, and a 'rack' to crisp the oatcakes before the fire. To keep oatcakes fresh they were buried in the meal girnel.

The iron pot which hung over the fire cooked porridge, simmered broths and stews, and was occasionally used as a primitive oven. The pot was laid over the fire, then glowing embers placed on the lid to heat the contents. One old recipe called 'black piece' perhaps describes the finished baked article!

Different oatcakes and bannocks were made to mark festivals and ward off evil. 'St Columba's cake', 'St Bride's bannock', 'Beltane bannock' and 'Yule bread' were baked for celebration and ritual, while others like the 'teethin' bannock' had a more practical use.

Early in the nineteenth century the introduction of the iron kitchen range, coupled with a drop in the price of sugar, tea and wheat, saw home baking flourish. Scottish hospitality is legendary, and now the housewife had the opportunity to hone her skills. She baked with what she had and it was not unusual for her to take 'baking' to be 'fired' at the local bakery. Work in service was common where exposure to a plethora of ingredients and recipes no doubt inspired many of the staff.

Scotland is a maritime nation, so inevitably trade and exploration introduced diverse food cultures. Settlers left by invasion or immigration brought their own culinary influence. It is to the Neolithic farmers that we must look to the beginnings of grain cultivation, milling on the stone quern and the start of baking. The Iron Age Celts' simple diet included sourdough bread often enriched with honey, and around the same time the invading Romans introduced spices, fruits and vegetables – mostly in the south. During the eighth century the Viking age brought Norse seafarers and traders with their barley flatbreads.

From around the early 1300s, Hanseatic merchants sailed northern trade routes, bringing dried fruit and spices to such ports as Cromarty in the north, to Leith in the south. From medieval times Aberdeen had close trading links with the Dutch. And who can forget the Italians who moved to Scotland after the First World War in search of work? Affectionately known as the 'Tallies' they brightened our lives with their good humour and cuisine. More recently Chinese, Asian, Polish and other nationalities have made Scotland their home and we wait to taste their influence in our kitchens.

The Auld Alliance with France has also left its mark, not least in 'Franco-Scottish' domestic terms, a fusion of French and Scots, which was an influence augmented by Mary, Queen of Scots, when she brought French cooks to Edinburgh in 1563. Mary was partial to thin, crisp shortbreads called 'petticoat tails', the name of which may be a corruption of 'petites gatelles' (little cakes) or due to their resemblance to the hooped petticoats worn by ladies at court. Shortbread originated in the medieval bakery where leftover dough was dried in the oven until it hardened to a 'biscuit'. In time butter replaced the yeast making the dough crumbly and 'short', with sugar added to sweeten it. However, the name bread – rather than biscuit or cake – remained.

The Bakers' Guild is one of the oldest. Baxters, as they were called, have baked commercially since the twelfth century. In 1364 King David II's household bought bread from a Dundee bakery, which suggests that bakeries were already established by that date. The Scottish Association of Master Bakers, formed in 1891, continues to support craft baking today.

Mary of Modena, the second wife of James II and VII (grandson of Mary, Queen of Scots), introduced tea drinking to Edinburgh in 1681 and by the early 1700s it became fashionable with women of the elite. Generally water was unsafe to drink so the population drank ale, claret, soor dook (butter milk) or fresh milk. Tea was an expensive luxury until 1894 when Gladstone repealed the tax levy. Tea drinking flourished. Women, from great ladies to farmers' wives, partook at 'four hours', which was soon renamed 'afternoon tea'. At first men rejected this new 'drink' but the lure of fresh home baking with an afternoon cuppa eventually won them over.

In the eighteenth century Glasgow became the largest importer of sugar in the UK, and that sugar being baked into biscuits, cakes, jams and sweeties no doubt encouraged the Scottish 'sweet tooth'. Scots referred to a slice of bread as a 'piece', which came to describe not only bread and jam but also a delicious cake or dainty. These would be known as a 'piece', 'fancy piece' or just a 'fancy'.

Miss Kate Cranston, a pioneer of social change, had the vision to create an enjoyable, affordable place for working folk to meet. She opened her first tea room in 1878 and soon her brilliant idea inspired others to do likewise. (The most famous are the restored Charles Rennie Mackintosh designed Willow Tea Rooms in Sauchiehall Street, Glasgow, originally opened in 1903.) Tea rooms were havens of leisure and taste where smart waitresses dressed in black, wearing white-frilled aprons and head bands, waited on customers seated at tables covered with pristine damask table cloths, appointed with the best china. Tea was served in gleaming silver-plated teapots along with the all-important three-tier cake stand. Bread, butter and sandwiches to start, followed by freshly baked scones and pancakes, and then the crowning glory of a selection of 'fancy pieces'. Oh, the fancies!

Afternoon or high tea? High tea was originally a meal served to working men between 3pm and 4pm, consisting of a form of hot cooked food followed by tea, scones and cakes. Eventually it was served in the early evening at a dining or high table, whereas afternoon tea would be taken earlier in the day, seated at leisure on comfortable chairs while delicacies were handed round from a lower table.

Founded in 1917, the Scottish WRI (now known as SWI) has done much to preserve and promote the heritage of Scottish baking. During the winter, baking competitions keep members on their mettle and in the summer county shows boast a baking tent where local talent is encouraged, tasted and judged. Long may this tradition continue.

Scots have settled in many parts of the world, and

wherever they landed there was one common denominator: a longing for home baking. Using ingredients at hand they recreated favourite recipes, and it is interesting to read cook books from those far-flung places to recognise the origins of those adapted 'pieces'.

Much has happened since those first bannocks baked on hot stones. It seems bere, that ancient grain, is a time capsule of interest to agronomists, for it holds the key to developing nutritious crops. Those early cereals of bere, oats and spelt wheat, which were baked by our forebears, are available once more and are easily incorporated in home baking to add nutrition and health benefits. Could this be 'bake' to the future?

The aim of this book is to give a glimpse into history along with easily made traditional recipes to bake and enjoy today. From bere bannocks to Aberdeen butteries and delicious biscuits to crunch and dunk; from indulgent lemon Madeira cake and light-as-a-feather strawberry sponge to wee fancies such as raspberry buns and 'sair heidies'.

The recipes are graded according to ease of making, with one rolling pin indicating a simple recipe, two for intermediate and three requiring more advanced skills. There are also hints and tips to encourage bakers of all ages.

Before you bake

1. Read the recipe. Collect utensils and ingredients.
2. Use scales or measuring spoons.
3. Use a timer. Tidy as you go.
4. Rice or gluten-free flour to dust is less sticky and easier to clean.
5. Break eggs individually into a cup so that a bad egg is easily discarded.
7. An alternative to buttermilk is full-cream milk soured with lemon juice – 1 tablespoon lemon juice to 150ml (¼ pint) milk.
8. To cut a rich cake, heat the knife in boiling water before each cut.
9. To incorporate ancient grains, replace up to 25 per cent of the flour with the same of an ancient grain such as bere barley, rye or spelt wheat.
10. Recipes suitable to bake gluten free using suitable ingredients are marked with **GF**
11. To prevent a cake rising to a peak in the middle, smooth the middle of the mixture with the back of the knuckles dipped in warm water.

Lining a cake tin

Use vegetable oil, a pastry brush, greaseproof paper, a pencil and scissors.

Draw twice round the base of the tin and cut out. Lay the paper flat, place the tin on its side at the edge, repeat to mark a strip twice the depth. Measure round the outside, add 10cm (4in) and cut the strip to that length. Fold in half

lengthwise, make a fold 2.5cm (1in) from the folded edge then cut 2.5cm (1in) into the second fold along the strip. Oil the tin and lay a paper base on the bottom. Ease the long strip round the inside, pressing the paper against the side with the cut folded piece flat on the base. Paint the join with oil, press together. Place the last base over this and brush the inside with oil.

Lining a loaf tin

Brush the tin with oil. Cut a strip of greaseproof paper to fit the base lengthwise, leaving the strip long enough to lift out the baked loaf.

The girdle

Rub with coarse salt or oil when cold. Wipe with a clean cloth to keep it non-stick. The girdle is at baking heat when flour sprinkled on the surface slowly turns golden brown. A thick-bottomed frying pan, electric girdle or crêpe maker are good alternatives.

Water icing

Some simple ideas to give a professional finish.

This quantity will cover an 18cm (7in) diameter cake
225g (8oz) sieved icing sugar
2 or 3 tablespoons water or fresh lemon juice

Sift the icing sugar into a bowl, add the liquid gradually (you may not need it all) and beat smooth. The consistency should coat the back of a wooden spoon. Add a few drops of colouring, if desired.

To ice a cake

To ice a cake heat a palette knife in hot water. Pour icing onto the centre of the cake, place the flat blade of the knife onto the icing while keeping the knife still. Gradually turn the cake plate, pressing lightly with the knife blade until the icing flows across the cake to the edges. Do not lift the knife, as this may lift the top off the cake and cause crumbs. Deftly turn the blade round the cake edge and lift off. Scatter with colourful icing sprinkles or try a feathered design.

Feather icing

Colour 1 tablespoon of icing and place in a piping bag with a fine writing nozzle.

Spread the cake with the rest of the icing then pipe lines about 2.5cm (1in) apart across the top. Drag the tip of a needle or skewer across the icing lines in one direction and then the other quickly before the icing sets to make the design. Looks very professional!

Bannocks, Bread and Scones

'God gives us the ingredients for our daily bread, but he expects us to do the baking!'

Chip Ingram, Christian pastor, author and teacher (1954)

Margaret Phillips' bere bannocks

Margaret lives in Mill Cottage opposite the Barony Mill at Birsay on Orkney where bere has been milled for generations. Her late husband Rae was the miller there.

Margaret bakes her bannocks with little wheat flour and mixes them with what she has – even home-brewed ale!

Makes 3 bannocks, 20cm (8in) diameter
350g (12oz) beremeal
115g (4oz) plain flour
Pinch of salt
2 teaspoons bicarbonate of soda
1 teaspoon cream of tartar
30g (1oz) margarine
1 tablespoon natural yoghurt
Milk and/or water, soured milk or ale to mix

Heat a girdle or thick-bottomed frying pan on low to medium heat. Sift the dry ingredients into a bowl, rub in the margarine and mix to a soft dough with the yoghurt and milk or other liquid. Turn onto a floured board, divide into three. Dust each with flour, pat out with the palm of your hand into a round about 20cm (8in) diameter and lift onto the hot girdle. Bake for 4 to 5 minutes on each side. Cool in a clean tea towel on a wire rack. Serve warm. Store sealed in a food bag for up to three days. Freeze for up to two months.

Baker's note

A bannock is one of the oldest healthiest breads; you can bake a quick version in the microwave.

Lay a sheet of kitchen towel on a flat microwavable plate, dust with beremeal, deposit a bannock onto the towel. Cover with a sheet of kitchen towel. Bake on high power for two minutes. Rest on the plate until firm enough to cool on a wire rack. Eat freshly baked.

Buttermilk bread

At one time buttermilk or 'soor dook' was drunk instead of water, which was often unsafe.

350g (12oz) plain flour
2 teaspoons cream of tartar
2 teaspoons bicarbonate of soda
1 teaspoon salt
115g (4oz) oatmeal plus 30g for dusting
30g (1oz) butter
360ml (12fl oz) buttermilk or soured milk (see page 21)

Heat the oven to 200°C (180°C fan), 400°F, Gas 6. Oil a large baking tray. Sift the flour, raising agents and salt into a bowl, add the oatmeal and rub in the butter. Make a hollow in the middle of the mix, pour in the buttermilk and mix lightly to a soft elastic dough. Dust the middle of the baking tray with oatmeal. Put the dough onto the baking tray then dust with oatmeal and flatten with the palm of your hand into a round 20cm (8in) diameter. Use the blade of a sharp knife to mark a cross over the top and prick lightly. Bake for 15 minutes in the middle of the oven then reduce the heat to 180°C (160°C fan), 350°F, Gas 4 for a further 5 to 10 minutes.

The bread is ready when it sounds hollow when knocked on the base with your knuckles. Remove from the oven and cool on a wire tray. Enjoy freshly baked.

Breakfast baps

A bap is a round, flattish bread roll. This recipe follows the tradition of fermenting the dough overnight so in the morning there are hot baps for breakfast!

Makes 8 to 10 baps
500g (1lb 2oz) strong white flour
7g (1 packet) dried yeast
2 level teaspoons salt
1 teaspoon sugar
390ml (14fl oz) tepid water
Rice flour to dust and roll out

The night before, sift the flour into a bowl and add the yeast, salt and sugar. Mix to a soft elastic dough with the tepid water. Use a dough hook or mix by hand for about 5 minutes. Put into a deep oiled bowl, cover with cling film and place on a low shelf in the fridge to prove overnight.

The next day, remove the dough from the fridge. Oil two baking trays. Turn the dough onto a floured surface, dust with flour and knead for five minutes until smooth. Divide into 8 or 10 pieces and knead each, pulling the top dough to the bottom to make a rounded dome. Lay on baking trays, cover with oiled polythene and prove in a warm place until doubled in size for anything up to 30 minutes. Meanwhile heat the oven to 240°C (220°C fan), 475°F, Gas 9. Dust the baps with bread or rice flour. Bake for 10 minutes then reduce heat to 200°C (180°C fan), 400°F, Gas 6 for 5 minutes. The baps are baked if they sound hollow when knocked on the base. Cool on a wire tray, eat freshly baked.

Baker's note
Dusting with flour helps develop a crust.

Annie's bread recipe

Annie was the chef at a well-known Worcestershire restaurant where the idea of this delicious loaf originates. I have altered the recipe a little to lighten the texture and make it easier to make.

Makes two large loaves – 750g (1lb 10oz)

300g (10oz) wholemeal bread flour
300g (10oz) white bread flour
60g (2oz) mixed seeds
7g (1 packet) dried yeast
10g (2 teaspoons) salt
20g (¾ oz) sugar
20g (¾ oz) lard melted with
    30g (1oz) black treacle
    500ml (16fl oz) dark beer
    Plus up to 50ml warm water

The night before, mix all the ingredients together to form a smooth dough, cover with cling film and leave in the fridge overnight to ferment. In the morning remove from the fridge and let the dough come up to room temperature. Turn onto a floured board and knead for about 5 minutes till smooth. Divide into two and shape into loaves. Try a pleat by rolling the dough into a long thick shape. Leaving one end attached, cut into three equal strips, pleat and seal at the end with a little water. Lay onto two oiled baking trays. Cover with a damp cloth and leave in a warm place for one hour to rise. Bake in a hot oven 220°C (200°C fan), 425°F, Gas 7 for about 10 minutes then reduce the heat to 200°C (180°C fan), 400°F, Gas 6 for a further 15 to 20 minutes. Till the base when knocked with the knuckles sounds hollow. Cool on a wire rack and enjoy freshly baked. Can be frozen.

Elgin-style butteries

A 'buttery' or 'Aberdeen rowie' is a North East speciality which bakers created for fishermen by adding fat and salt to bread dough so that rolls kept well and provided an energy boost. My friend Maureen bakes this Elgin baker's recipe when she visits her daughter in Canada.

Makes 16 large or 20 smaller butteries
7g (1 packet) dried yeast or 60g (2oz) fresh yeast
1 tablespoon caster sugar
450ml (15 fl oz) warm water
500g (1lb 2oz) strong white flour
Pinch of salt
125g (4½ oz) butter or margarine
250g (9oz) lard
Rice flour

The night before, mix the yeast and sugar with a little warm water. Set aside. Mix the flour and salt in a large bowl. Once the yeast has bubbled, add this with the remaining water and mix to a smooth dough. Cover with cling film and place in the fridge overnight.

The next day, remove the dough from the fridge. Oil three baking trays. Cream the butter and lard together. Turn the dough onto a board dusted with rice flour and knead for 5 minutes. Using your hands gradually press the fat mix into the dough, working it in

as you knead until it is evenly blended. Allow to rest for
40 minutes. Cut roughly into 16 pieces. Shape each into
a rough circle, place on the baking trays and set aside in a
cool place to rise for 45 minutes. Meanwhile heat the
oven to 200°C (180°C fan), 400°F, Gas 6. Bake for 10 to
15 minutes until light golden brown and slightly crispy.
Cool on a wire tray.

Baker's note
To make a 'healthier' buttery reduce the fat by 25 per
cent. Substitute 100g oatmeal for 100g flour.

A good oven scone

The secret of a good scone is to make the dough as soft as you can handle – do so as little as possible. Bake quickly in a hot oven.

Makes 6 × 7.5cm (3in) or 9 × 6cm (2½ in) round scones
250g (9oz) self-raising flour
1 teaspoon baking powder
1 teaspoon caster sugar
60g (2oz) butter, cubed
1 large egg, beaten
150ml (¼ pint) milk

Heat the oven to 230°C (210°C fan), 450°F, Gas 8. Oil a baking tray. Sift the flour and baking powder into a bowl, add the sugar and rub in the butter. Add the egg with sufficient milk to make a soft elastic dough. Turn onto a floured board. Dust with flour and pat out gently using the palm of your hand to 2.5cm (1in) thick. Cut into rounds with a floured cutter and lay on the oiled tray, leaving room for the scones to expand. Gently knead trimmings together and repeat. Bake for 10 to 12 minutes until risen, golden on top and the base when knocked with the knuckles sounds hollow. Cool on a wire rack. Eat freshly baked.

Baker's note
Add grated apple and cinnamon or grated lemon rind with a few fresh blueberries to the uncooked scone dough.

An easy scone for beginners, like my friend Irene:
Dust the baking tray with flour. Turn the dough onto the middle of the tray, dust with flour and pat into a round about 3.5cm (1½ in) thick. Mark into four with a knife. Bake for 10 to 12 minutes until risen, golden and firm. Cool on the tray until firm enough to cool on a wire rack. Break in four and enjoy warm.

Girdle or soda scones

One of my late father's treats which he enjoyed, warm from the girdle, smothered in home-made raspberry jam.

Makes 8 scones
225g (8oz) plain flour
½ teaspoon salt
¼ teaspoon bicarbonate of soda
2 teaspoons baking powder
150ml (¼ pint) buttermilk or soured milk (see page 21)

Heat the girdle or a thick-bottomed frying pan on low to medium heat. Sift the dry ingredients into a bowl, make a well in the middle and pour in the buttermilk. Mix to a soft elastic dough, adding a little more milk if required. Turn out onto a floured board and divide in two. Pat out into two rounds about 5mm (¼ in) thick and cut each into four triangles. Bake on the girdle for 5 to 6 minutes on each side. Cool on a wire rack, wrapped in a clean tea towel.

The ultimate cheese scone

All tasters agreed this is a winner. A recipe by home baker Kath Donaldson, who plays the keyboard with our local band the Greenbrae Gaugers.

Makes 6 × 7.5cm (3in) scones
175g (6oz) self-raising flour
1 teaspoon baking powder
¼ teaspoon salt
45g (1½ oz) butter
85g (3oz) grated mature cheddar cheese
1 egg, beaten
Milk

Heat the oven to 200°C (180°C fan), 400°F, Gas 6. Oil a baking tray. Sift the dry ingredients into a bowl and rub in the butter. Stir in the cheese, leaving some to sprinkle on the scones. Mix to a soft elastic dough with the egg and milk, leaving a little to brush the tops. Turn onto a floured board, dust the top with flour then pat out to 2cm (¾ in) thickness. Cut into rounds, brush with egg, scatter with cheese and place on the baking tray. Bake for 12 to 15 minutes until risen and golden and the base sounds hollow to a tap from the knuckles. Cool on a wire tray. Best eaten warm and freshly baked.

Katie's drop scones

My late neighbour Katie Miller came from the island of Barra where she was brought up on home-baking. Her recipe includes syrup and melted butter which bakes a soft golden scone.

Makes 10 to 12 drop scones
115g (4oz) self-raising flour
35g (1 generous oz) golden syrup
1 egg
90ml (3fl oz) milk
1 level teaspoon baking powder
15g (0.5oz) melted butter

Heat a girdle or thick-bottomed frying pan on low to medium heat. Sift the flour into a bowl, add the egg and syrup then beat to a softly thick dropping batter with the milk. I use a balloon whisk. Stir in the melted butter along with the baking powder. Test the heat of the girdle (see p. 23), rub with oil, drop tablespoons of batter onto the surface and leave to set till bubbles begin to burst on the uncooked surface. Flip over with the flat blade of a palette knife or fish slice to cook the other side, gently tap the cooked side releasing any trapped air for an even bake on the underside. Cool on a wire rack, wrapped in a clean tea towel. Enjoy freshly baked with butter, honey, jam or lemon curd. The scones freeze well for up to 6 weeks.

Aberdeen crulla

There was once a strong Dutch connection with Aberdeen so 'crulla' may come from the Dutch 'krullen', meaning a scroll.

Makes 12 to 14 crulla
60g (2oz) butter
60g (2oz) caster sugar
225g (8oz) self-raising flour
1 teaspoon cinnamon
2 eggs, beaten
Oil to deep fry
Rice flour to knead and shape

Sift the flour and cinnamon into a bowl. Cream the butter and sugar. Stir in the dry ingredients along with the eggs to make a soft pliable dough. Knead until smooth on a floured board. Divide into 12 or 14 equal pieces. Roll each into a long sausage shape about 10cm (4in) long. Cut the roll lengthwise into three equal strips, leaving them joined at one end. Plait the strips and seal the end with a little water. Heat the oil in a deep-fat pan or frier on low to medium heat and test with a small piece of dough. If it sizzles and turns golden the oil is ready to cook. Do not overheat because the outside will cook quickly leaving the inside raw. Cook in small batches, three or four at a time, turning to ensure even browning. Lift onto kitchen towel to drain, toss in caster sugar and eat freshly baked.

Biscuits

'The secret of a good biscuit is an empty plate.'

John Smith (Baker, New Pitsligo) affectionately
known as 'Biscuit John'

Highland oatcakes

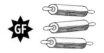

Highland oatcakes are made purely of oatmeal. Mix one round at a time, as the mixture dries soon after mixing. Be quick!

Makes 8 large triangle oatcakes
100g (3½ oz) medium oatmeal
Generous pinch of salt and the same of bicarbonate of soda
10 ml (2 teaspoons) sunflower oil
Water to mix
Oatmeal or rice flour to dust

Heat the oven to 180°C (160°C fan), 350°F, Gas 4. Oil a baking tray. Measure dry ingredients into a bowl and add the oil. Stir in enough tepid water to make a soft, clean, pliable dough. Knead smooth on a board dusted with oatmeal or rice flour. Roll out into a thin round and divide into eight triangles. Lay onto the baking tray and bake for 15 to 20 minutes until crisp and beginning to curl at the edges. Cool on a wire rack. Store in an airtight container.

Baker's note
Weigh out several batches in separate bowls and keep mixing, rolling and baking!

One round is called a bannock and the triangles are known as farls.

Seaweed nibbles

Makes 24

Add two or three teaspoons of dried kelp or seaweed crisps to the above mix.

Roll the dough into a thin square and cut into 5cm (2in) squares. Bake for 10 minutes until crisp. Cool and store as above.

Old-fashioned butter biscuits

First made commercially by Forbes Simmer at his bakery
in the Aberdeenshire village of Hatton, which he began
in 1888 with £60 and a borrowed horse. My father loved
them, two at a time, as 'biscuit butter and shut'!

Makes 24 × 7.5cm (3in) biscuits
225g (8oz) plain flour
1 teaspoon salt
½ teaspoon bicarbonate of soda
100g (3½ oz) butter, softened
Water to mix – about 2 tablespoons

Heat the oven to 180°C (160°C fan), 350°F, Gas 4. Grease
three baking trays. Sift the flour, salt and bicarbonate of
soda into a bowl, add the butter and rub in. Mix with
tepid water to a soft smooth dough. Knead lightly on a
floured board and roll out to 3mm (⅛ in) thickness and
cut into rounds. Place on the baking trays and prick
twice in the middle of the biscuit. Bake for 12 to 15
minutes until golden and firm to touch. Cool on a wire
tray. Store in an airtight container for up to two weeks.

Baker's note
Add cheese and this biscuit becomes a moreish nibble!
Change the recipe slightly using 75g (2½ oz) butter and
45g (1½ oz) grated cheddar, mix with a beaten egg.
Method as above.

digestive biscuits

...estive biscuit was developed in 1839 by ...ctors who believed that the addition of ...onate aided digestion – hence the name 'digestive ... s still the UK's best-selling biscuit.

Makes 18 to 20 × 5cm (2in) biscuits
85g (3oz) butter or margarine
30g (1oz) soft brown sugar
115g (4oz) spelt or wholemeal flour
115g (4oz) medium oatmeal
¼ teaspoon bicarbonate of soda
1 teaspoon baking powder
Milk to mix

Heat the oven to 180°C (160°C fan), 350°F, Gas 4. Oil two baking trays. Cream the butter and sugar until light. Add the dry ingredients and mix to a stiff, clean dough adding a little milk if needed. Roll out to 5mm (¼ in) thickness and cut into rounds with a fluted cutter. Lay on the baking trays and bake for 12 to 15 minutes until crisp. Cool a little on the tray and then on a wire rack. Store in an airtight container for up to two weeks.

Baker's note
Adding cracked black pepper makes a delicious biscuit for cheese. Chocolate chips transform the plain biscuit into an indulgent one.

Empire biscuits

These traditional Scottish dainties were originally known in the UK as Deutsche or German biscuits. During the First World War the name was changed to Empire biscuits. In Canada they are known as Imperial biscuits.

Makes 12 biscuits
115g (4oz) butter
115g (4oz) caster sugar
225g (8oz) plain flour
½ teaspoon baking powder
1 level teaspoon ground cinnamon
1 small egg, beaten
Raspberry jam
Water icing (see page 23)
6 glacé cherries, halved

Heat the oven to 180°C (160°C fan), 350°F, Gas 4. Oil two baking trays. Cream the butter and sugar until light. Sift in the flour, baking powder and cinnamon and stir in gradually with enough egg to make a soft, pliable dough. Roll out to 3mm (⅛ in) thickness and cut into biscuits about 5cm (2in) diameter using a fluted cutter. Bake for 15 to 20 minutes until golden and crisp. Cool on a wire tray. When cool spread half the biscuits with jam, place the others on top, then spread with water icing and finish by adding a piece of cherry in the centre.

Baker's note

An easy way to spread icing onto the biscuits is to use the back of a teaspoon in one hand while holding the biscuit in the other.

Shortbread

A good basic recipe I learned at school, based on one from *The Glasgow Cookery Book*. The addition of cornflour gives a smooth mouth texture to the biscuit.

**Makes 12 to 14 fingers of shortbread or 24 round biscuits
5cm (2in) diameter**

115g (4oz) butter
60g (2oz) caster sugar
175g (6oz) plain flour
30g (1oz) cornflour

Heat the oven to 160°C (140°C fan), 325°F, Gas 3. Cream the butter and sugar until light. Sift the dry ingredients into the creamed mixture and mix together to make a smooth, pliable dough. Knead until smooth on a floured board, then roll out to 5mm (¼ in) thickness and cut into rounds. Alternatively roll into a long strip about 10cm (4in) wide, pinch round the edges with thumb and forefinger, then cut into strips about 2cm (¾ in) wide. Bake for 20 to 25 minutes until golden and crisp. Cool on the try a little and dust with caster sugar while warm. Store in an airtight container, up to 2 weeks.

Baker's note
A tip from my friend Helen is to replace the cornflour with semolina which makes a crunchier biscuit.

Tantallon cakes

A lemon-flavoured shortbread biscuit named after
Tantallon Castle near North Berwick. Brodies, a local
baker, sold these biscuits from a large glass jar on the
counter labelled 'Tantallon Teacakes'. The Royal family
were said to enjoy them.

Makes 26 biscuits approximately 7.5cm (3in) diameter

115g (4oz) butter
60g (2oz) caster sugar
30g (1oz) icing sugar
Grated rind of 1 lemon
150g (5oz) plain flour
85g (3oz) cornflour
½ teaspoon bicarbonate of soda
1 egg, beaten

Heat the oven to 180°C (160°C fan), 350°F, Gas 4. Grease
three baking trays. Cream the butter and sugars until
light. Stir in the lemon rind along with the flours and
bicarbonate of soda, adding the beaten egg to make a soft
smooth dough. Knead a little on a floured board, roll out
to 5mm (¼ in) thick and cut into rounds with a fluted
cutter. Place on the prepared baking trays and prick the
middle of each biscuit with a fork. Bake for 15 to 20
minutes until golden and crisp. Cool a little on the tray,
dust with caster sugar then complete cooling on a wire
rack. Store in an airtight container for up to two weeks.

Raspberry oat shortbread

Created in memory of my baker friend and mentor, the late John Smith, who was one of the last of the famous baking family Smiths of New Pitsligo. Affectionately known as 'Biscuit John', he won several awards for his raspberry and blueberry shortbreads.

Makes 28 biscuits 5cm (2in) diameter
150g (5oz) softened butter
85g (3oz) caster sugar
1 teaspoon of raspberry extract or a few drops of raspberry essence
150g (5oz) rolled oats
115g (4oz) plain flour
1 teaspoon baking powder
45g (1½ oz) fresh or frozen raspberries, crushed

Heat the oven to 180°C (160°C fan), 350°F, Gas 4. Oil three baking trays. Cream the butter and sugar until light, beat in the raspberry essence, stir in the dry ingredients and lastly the raspberries. Turn onto a floured board and knead a little. Roll out to 5mm (¼ in) thickness and cut into rounds with a fluted cutter. Bake for 15 to 20 minutes until crisp and lightly coloured. Cool on a wire rack and store in an airtight container for up to two weeks.

Home-made custard creams

Invented in 1908, this fancy biscuit soon became a national favourite. It remains fourth in the biscuit-selling league and it is reckoned that 25 tonnes are made each day. In some areas the home-made variety are called 'yoyos'.

Makes approximately 12 custard creams

115g (4oz) self-raising flour
85g (3oz) caster sugar
85g (3oz) custard powder
1 teaspoon baking powder
115g (4oz) butter or margarine
1 egg, beaten
1 teaspoon vanilla essence (optional)

Heat the oven to 180°C (160°C fan), 350°F, Gas 4. Oil two baking trays. Mix all the dry ingredients together and rub in the butter or margarine until the mix resembles fine breadcrumbs. Mix with beaten egg to make a stiff smooth dough. Roll out to 5mm (¼ in) thickness. Cut in rounds 6cm (2in) diameter and bake for 10 to 15 minutes until risen and set. Cool a little on the tray then on a wire rack. When cold, sandwich together with vanilla buttercream icing (see page 58).

Next time you eat a custard cream, note the intricate
Victorian pattern, which was so attractive to the first
biscuit buyers.

This recipe comes from Miss N. Gordon and was printed
in a local church recipe book dated 1971.

Gypsy creams

There are, I discovered, several schools of thought as to the construction of the authentic gypsy cream biscuit. I leave you to try your own version.

Makes 28 biscuits
60g (2oz) butter or margarine
60g (2oz) lard or vegetable shortening
85g (3oz) caster sugar
1 dessertspoon golden syrup
1 dessertspoon hot water
1 teaspoon vanilla essence
115g (4oz) self-raising flour
115g (4oz) porridge oats
½ teaspoon bicarbonate of soda

Heat the oven to 180°C (160°C fan), 350°F, Gas 4. Oil two baking trays. Cream the fats and sugar until light, then beat in the syrup dissolved in the hot water along with the vanilla essence. Stir in the remaining ingredients to make a stiff mixture. Place teaspoons of the mixture well apart on the baking trays and bake for 12 to 15 minutes until firm and golden. Cool a little on the trays then on a wire rack. Store in an airtight container. Sandwich together with vanilla or chocolate buttercream (see page 58).

Baker's note
If you prefer a chocolate-flavoured biscuit add
2 teaspoons cocoa powder to the flour before mixing.

Basic buttercream

115g (4oz) unsalted butter
270g (9½ oz) sifted icing sugar
2 or 3 tablespoons full-fat milk

Cream the butter for 4 to 5 minutes until pale and increased in volume. Scrape down the bowl. Add half the icing sugar. Stir on very low speed to mix and avoid clouds of sugar! Beat on high for 4 to 5 minutes then repeat. The icing will be quite stiff. To loosen the consistency beat in up to 3 tablespoons of milk. Refrigerate in a sealed container up to one week or freeze for one month.

Add flavour like vanilla or other essence, or colour. For chocolate buttercream beat in melted chocolate or cocoa powder to taste.

Melting moments

Promoted by the Be-Ro flour company in 1930, these biscuits then known as MMs have become a national favourite. Over the years bakers have made their own version of the recipe. Here are two from my collection.

The cornflake variety

Handwritten in a family cookbook.

45g (1½ oz) butter or margarine
75g (2½ oz) lard
85g (3oz) caster sugar
150g (5oz) self-raising flour
60g (2oz) crushed cornflakes
1 small egg, beaten

Heat the oven to 180°C (160°C fan), 350°F, Gas 4. Oil three baking trays. Cream the fat and sugar together until light. Stir in the flour and cornflakes with enough beaten egg to bind to a soft dough. Place heaped teaspoons on the trays leaving room for the biscuits to spread as they bake. Flatten gently with the back of a fork and bake in the oven for 12 to 15 minutes until golden. Cool a little on the tray then on a wire rack. Store in an airtight container, up to 2 weeks.

Baker's note

Some bakers like to top each biscuit with a quarter of a glacé cherry before baking. Other recipes add a dessertspoon of custard powder to the mixture.

The oat variety

Adapted from the original Be-Ro recipe.

45g (1½ oz) lard
75g (2½ oz) margarine
85g (3oz) caster sugar
150g (5oz) self-raising flour
45g (1½ oz) rolled oats, plus more to coat
Beaten egg
Glacé cherries cut into quarters

Heat the oven to 180°C (160°C fan), 350°F, Gas 4. Oil two baking trays. Cream the fats and sugar, then stir in the dry ingredients with enough egg to make a firm but soft consistency. Roll into balls the size of a small walnut, roll in oats, and place on the trays. Top with a quarter cherry. Bake for 15 to 20 minutes until golden. Cool a little on the tray then on a wire rack. Store in an airtight container for up to three weeks.

Traditional Scotch perkins

A perkin is similar in name to its softer Yorkshire cousin, parkin, but is in fact a crisp oatmeal biscuit. This recipe is from Orcadian baker friend Stewart McConnach.

Makes 30 biscuits
150g (5oz) plain flour
5g (1 teaspoon) each of ground cinnamon and mixed spice
7.5g (1½ teaspoons) ground ginger
10g (2 teaspoons) bicarbonate of soda
150g (5oz) medium oatmeal
75g (2½ oz) caster sugar
Pinch of salt
85g (3oz) butter
120g (4¼ oz) golden syrup, warmed

Heat the oven to 180°C (160°C fan), 350°F, Gas 4. Oil three baking trays. Sift the flour, spices and bicarbonate of soda into a bowl. Add oatmeal, sugar and salt. Rub in the butter. Stir in the warm syrup to make a pliable dough. Leave to rest for 5 to 10 minutes. Roll out on a floured board to 3mm (⅛ in) thickness. Cut into 6cm (2½ in) rounds and lay on the trays with room for the biscuit to spread. Bake for 12 to 15 minutes till golden and set. Watch them, because perkins burn easily. Cool a little on the tray then cool on a wire rack. Store in an airtight container, up to 2 weeks.

Baker's note

For a spicier perkin, add another 2.5g (½ teaspoon) ground ginger.

Uncle George's biscuits

It seems that Uncle George is no relation to the friend who gave me this recipe, which is baked from Fife to Moray and beyond. But who was Uncle George, I wonder?

Makes 36 biscuits

115g (4oz) soft butter
115g (4oz) caster sugar
60g (2oz) chopped mixed nuts
175g (6oz) self-raising flour
1 dessertspoon syrup (approx 20g)
½ teaspoon bicarbonate of soda

Heat the oven to 180°C (160°C fan), 350°F, Gas 4. Oil three baking trays. Cream the butter and caster sugar. Stir in the remaining ingredients and mix well. Place in balls the size of a walnut on the trays, leaving room for the biscuit to spread. Bake for 15 to 20 minutes until dark golden. Do not overbake – this mix burns easily. Cool on the tray for a few minutes, then loosen with a palette knife and lift on a wire rack to cool. Store in an airtight container, 7–10 days.

Fatty cutties

This recipe from the northern isles is a delicious 'almost biscuit' made on a girdle.

Makes 18 to 20
115g (4oz) butter or margarine
60g (2oz) caster sugar
175g (6oz) plain flour sifted with
    a pinch of bicarbonate of soda
60g (2oz) currants

Heat the girdle on low heat. Cream the butter and sugar, add the dry ingredients and mix to a soft clean dough. Turn the dough onto a floured board and knead well. Form into an oblong and divide into three. Dust each with flour and roll out thinly to an even strip 10cm (4in) wide. Cut into six or seven fingers about 3.25cm (1½ in) wide. Repeat. Test the heat of the girdle (see page xx). Fatty cutties burn easily, so better to keep it on the low side for heat. Bake for about 3 minutes on each side until pale golden, turning once. Cool on a wire rack. Store in an airtight container, 7–10 days.

Waffle biscuits

A recipe from my childhood which Mum made to 'fill the tins'.

Makes 12 biscuits
60g (2oz) soft brown sugar
60g (2oz) golden syrup
60g (2oz) lard or white fat
60g (2oz) butter or margarine
¼ teaspoon bicarbonate of soda
175g (6oz) self-raising flour
½ teaspoon ground ginger

Heat the oven to 180°C (160°C fan), 350°F, Gas 4. Oil two baking trays. Melt the first four ingredients in a saucepan. Sift the flour and ginger into a bowl. Stir the bicarbonate of soda into the melted mixture until it froths, then stir in the flour to make a smooth sticky dough. Place teaspoons on the trays leaving space for the biscuits to spread. Flatten with a fork to make a waffle pattern. Bake for 12 to 15 minutes. Cool a little on the tray then on a wire rack. Store in an airtight container, 7–10 days.

Lemon shorties

Another childhood favourite from the baking tins!

Makes 16 to 18 biscuits
115g (4oz) butter or margarine
60g (2oz) icing sugar
Grated rind of 1 lemon
115g (4oz) self-raising flour

Heat the oven to 180°C (160°C fan), 350°F, Gas 4. Oil
two baking trays. Cream the butter and sugar, then stir in
the lemon rind and flour. Place teaspoons of mixture on
the trays leaving room between each as the biscuits will
spread. Bake for 12 to 15 minutes. Cool on a wire rack.
When cold, ice the tops with a lemon water icing
(see page 23).

Pastries, Tarts and Traybakes

'To beat the Edinburgh baker, you must go — not to London, but to Paris or Vienna.'

T.F. Henderson, *Old World Scotland*

Sausage rolls

Each New Year my mother made sausage rolls with shortcrust pastry. They are delicious.

Makes 12 sausage rolls

Pastry:
225g (8oz) plain flour
Pinch of salt
60g (2oz) butter or margarine
60g (2oz) lard or white fat
Cold water

Sift the flour and salt into a bowl. Rub in the fats and mix with enough cold water to make a stiff elastic dough. Knead until smooth and rest the dough while you prepare the sausages.

---

6 large pork or beef sausages, skinned
Beaten egg

Heat the oven to 190°C (170°C fan), 375°F, Gas 5. Oil a baking tray. Roll the pastry into an oblong about 30cm (12in) long and 15cm (6in) wide. Skin the sausages and roll together in a little flour to make one long sausage to fit the length of the pastry. Lay this 5cm (1in) from the edge. Brush the remaining pastry with egg or water then roll the narrow edge of the pastry over the sausage onto the egged part to seal and make a long roll. Divide into twelve equal pieces, lay on the prepared tray, cut two sort slashes in the top of each and brush with beaten egg. Bake for 15 to 20 minutes until golden. Enjoy hot or cold.

Baker's note
As an alternative, use puff pastry (see page 71). For vegans, omit egg, use vegan sausages and fat.

Cheese d'Artois

This family favourite is from *The Glasgow Cookery Book* awarded to my mother as first prize at Hyndland public school in 1940. One of Mum's standbys and very tasty it is too.

Puff pastry:
225g (8oz) plain flour
¼ teaspoon salt
75g (2½ oz) margarine or butter
75g (2½ oz) lard or white fat
Squeeze of lemon juice
Cold water

Sift the dry ingredients into a bowl. Cut the fat into small pieces. Mix into the flour with enough cold water to make a stiff dough. Roll into a strip on a floured board, fold over one third from the top and then from the bottom to make a square. Seal the edges with the rolling pin and turn the dough once. Roll out and repeat three times or as often as required to mix in the fat. Rest the pastry for half an hour before use.

Filling:
85g (3oz) grated cheddar cheese
30g (1oz) melted butter
1 large egg, beaten
Salt, pepper and a pinch of cayenne pepper

Heat the oven to 200°C (180°C fan), 400°F, Gas 6. Divide pastry in two. Roll each to approximately 20cm × 25cm (8in × 10in). Lay one square on an oiled baking tin. Mix the filling ingredients, retaining a little beaten egg to brush the top. Spread the filling on the pastry, leaving about 5mm (¼ in) round the sides. Wet the edges and lay on the second square of pastry. Press the edges together. Brush with egg and bake in a hot oven for 10 to 15 minutes until golden. Cool a little, cut into fingers and serve warm.

Baker's note
For speed, use ready-made puff pastry.

Home-made bacon and egg pie

A bacon and egg pie can be fiddly to make. This easier
alternative came from a 1950s cookery demonstration
held in the local hydroelectric offices to teach
housewives how to use new electric appliances!

Makes an 18cm (7in) pie

Shortcrust pastry:
225g (8oz) plain flour
¼ teaspoon salt
60g (2oz butter
60g (2oz) lard
Cold water to mix

Sift the dry ingredients into a bowl. Rub in the fats and
mix with enough cold water to make a stiff elastic
dough. Knead until smooth and rest the dough while
you prepare the filling.

Filling:
1 small tin (225g) sweetcorn, drained
225g (8oz) back bacon, chopped
45g (1½ oz) grated cheddar cheese
2 large eggs beaten with
    120ml (4fl oz) milk and
    Salt and ground black pepper
    Dash of Tabasco or Worcester sauce

Heat the oven to 190°C (170°C fan), 375°F, Gas 5. Use two thirds of the pastry to line a flan dish 20cm (8in) diameter. Scatter the chopped bacon, sweetcorn and cheese over the base. Pour the beaten egg and milk over, retaining a little to brush the pastry top. Roll out the remaining pastry to cover the flan dish. Wet the edges of the pie base, cover with the pastry and pinch the edges between the thumb and forefinger to seal. Brush with the beaten egg. Make two slits in the lid to let steam escape. Bake for 30 to 35 minutes until golden and set. Serve hot or cold.

Baker's note
Make a quiche topped with cheese and sliced tomato instead of pastry. Use pastry scraps to make wee cheese tarts. Line a muffin tin, half fill each with grated cheese and cover with beaten egg and milk.

Paradise cake

A recipe from a dear friend affectionately known as 'Sis', who looked after us as children. A fusion of Border tart recipes, sometimes called Mallorcan slice – perhaps a reference to holidays on that island when travel became easier during the 1950s.

Makes 2 × 18cm (7in) tarts

Pastry base:
175g (6oz) plain flour
85g (3oz) butter
1 egg yolk
Water

Filling:
115g (4oz) butter
115g (4oz) caster sugar
1 egg, plus the white left from the pastry
30g (1oz) ground rice
60g (2oz) ground almonds
Raspberry jam
45g (1½ oz) chopped glacé cherries
45g (1½ oz) chopped walnuts
115g (4oz) sultanas
Caster sugar to dust

Heat the oven to 180°C (160°C fan) 350°F, Gas 4. Oil two sandwich tins. First make the pastry. Sift the flour into a bowl and rub in the butter. Stir in the egg yolk and enough water to make a stiff, smooth dough. Knead a little on a floured board. Halve the dough and roll out to line each of the tins. Spread the base of each with jam.

Make the filling by creaming the butter and sugar until light, beat in the egg and egg white, and stir in the rest of the ingredients. Divide between the two tins and spread evenly over the pastry. Bake for 20 minutes, then reduce the heat to 160°C (140°C fan), 325°F, Gas 3 for a further 10 minutes or until the filling is risen and firm to touch. Cool a little and dust with caster sugar. Cool in the tins and enjoy freshly baked.

Apple coffee cake

From a baking book compiled by the Birsay Lifeboat Ladies Guild. I noticed the absence of coffee in the ingredients and checked with a member. 'The cake is baked to enjoy with coffee,' was the answer.

85g (3oz) butter
115g (4oz) caster sugar
1 teaspoon vanilla essence
2 eggs, beaten
225g (8oz) self-raising flour
1 teaspoon baking powder
½ teaspoon bicarbonate of soda
¼ teaspoon salt
225g (8oz) soured cream
175g (6oz) chopped apples

Topping:
115g (4oz) self-raising flour
85g (3oz) soft brown sugar
60g (2oz) butter, melted
1 teaspoon cinnamon
85g (3oz) chopped pecan nuts

Heat the oven to 180°C (160°C fan), 350°F, Gas 4.
Oil and line a deep baking tin approx 23cm × 30cm
(9in × 12in). Cream the butter and sugar together till
light, add vanilla essence and eggs and beat well. Sift the
dry ingredients into a bowl and add alternately with the
cream stirring to a smooth batter. Stir in the apples.
Spread evenly over the base of the baking tin. Mix the
topping ingredients together and scatter over the cake
base. Bake in the middle of the oven for 30 to 35 minutes
till risen and firm. Cool in the tin. Cut into slices and
enjoy freshly baked.

Netta Wyllie's fruit slices

Netta's home bakes are well known on Orkney, where local beremeal adds flavour. She kindly shared this favourite recipe. My family call these 'fly cemeteries' perhaps due to the currants in the filling!

Makes 24 slices – Swiss roll tin 20cm × 25cm (8in × 10in)

Filling:
175g (6oz) currants
175g (6oz) sultanas
240ml (8 fl oz) water
1 teaspoon mixed spice
85g (3oz) demerara sugar
60g (2oz) margarine or butter
3 teaspoons cornflour slaked with a little water

Put the fruit, water, spice, sugar and margarine into a pan and bring to the boil. Thicken with cornflour, stirring till the mix thickens. Turn off the heat and cool.

Rich pastry:
175g (6oz) plain flour
175g (6oz) beremeal (or plain flour)
175g (6oz) butter
15g (½ oz) caster sugar
1 egg yolk
Water, if needed to mix

Heat the oven to 180°C (160°C fan), 350°F, Gas 4. Sift the flour into a bowl and rub in the butter. Stir in the sugar. Mix in the egg yolk and enough cold water to make a smooth dough. Roll two-thirds of the pastry to line the tin. Spread evenly with the fruit mix. Cover with the rest of the pastry and bake for 25 to 30 minutes until golden. Dust with caster sugar when hot. Cut into 24 squares while warm. Cool in the tin. Store in a sealed container for up to a week.

Alison's mocha squares

A recipe from my friend Alison. A delicious cross between a chocolate brownie and a flapjack. One to return to as a quick standby traybake.

Makes a 20cm (8in) square tin
225g (8oz) butter or margarine
225g (8oz) granulated sugar
225g (8oz) self-raising flour
150g (5oz) porridge oats
60g (2oz) cocoa powder

Heat the oven to 180°C (160°C fan), 350°F, Gas 4. Oil the baking tin. Melt the butter in a large pan, add the other ingredients and mix well. Press evenly into the prepared tin and bake for 15 minutes. Remove from the oven and cool in the tin. Spread with the topping when cold.

Topping:
225g (8oz) icing sugar
60g (2oz) butter or margarine
1 dessertspoon instant coffee dissolved in 1 tablespoon boiling water

---

Melt the butter and stir in the other ingredients. Pour over the baked mixture. Cut in squares when set. Store in an airtight container for up to one week.

Broken biscuit cake

At one time bakers and grocers sold loose biscuits. Broken ones bought cheaply were often used to make an economical 'no-cook' cake.

115g (4oz) butter
30g (1oz) caster sugar
2 tablespoons cocoa powder
2 tablespoons golden syrup
2 tablespoons milk
250g (8oz) plain biscuits like digestives or rich tea, crushed
60g (2oz) chopped walnuts or hazelnuts
30g (1oz) sultanas
30g (1oz) chopped glacé cherries

Oil a 20cm (8in) square baking tin. Line the base with greaseproof paper. Melt the butter in a pan. Stir in sugar, cocoa, syrup and milk, then add the remaining ingredients. Pour into the tin, smooth the top with the back of a tablespoon. Leave to cool and set. Cut into fingers.

Baker's note
To crush biscuits, place in a polythene bag, seal the top and bash with a rolling pin or wooden spoon.

Add chopped marshmallows to the mixture for an extra treat.

Date slices

A simple recipe to make your own. Some add coconut or chopped nuts, others lemon or orange rind to the filling. What will you bake?

Makes 24 small slices or 16 larger ones

Base:
115g (4oz) self-raising flour
½ teaspoon bicarbonate of soda
115g (4oz) rolled oats
115g (4oz) butter
115g (4oz) caster sugar

Filling:
225g (8oz) chopped dates
150ml (¼ pint) water
1 teaspoon vanilla essence

Heat the oven to 180°C (160°C fan), 350°F, Gas 4. Oil a Swiss roll tin 20cm × 23cm (8in × 9in). Cook the dates in water until soft, stirring to prevent sticking. Turn off the heat, cool, stir in the vanilla essence. Sift the flour and bicarbonate of soda into a bowl, add the oats then rub in the butter. Press half the mixture into the base of the prepared tin. Pour the stewed dates over and spread evenly. Scatter the remaining oat mixture over the dates and press down gently. Bake for 20 to 25 minutes until golden and set. Cool in the tin. Mark into squares while warm. Enjoy freshly baked or keep for up to a week in an airtight container.

Baker's note
At Christmas substitute dates with mincemeat.

Raspberry and apple flapjack

A traybake with possibilities. Add seeds, dried fruits, lemon or orange rind, even chocolate chips! Fresh fruit gives a chewy texture.

Makes a 20cm × 23cm (8in × 9in) tin
115g (4oz) butter
85g (3oz) syrup
85g (3oz) soft brown sugar
280g (10oz) rolled oats
60g (2oz) crushed raspberries
60g (2oz) grated apple

Heat the oven to 180°C (160°C fan), 350°F, Gas 4. Oil the baking tin. Melt butter, syrup and sugar in a saucepan and stir in the remaining ingredients. Turn into the tin and spread evenly. Bake for 25 minutes until golden and set. Cool in the tin. Mark into squares while warm. Store in an airtight container for up to two weeks.

Dark chocolate orange fudge squares

A different take on the old favourite 'millionaire's shortbread' made with Scottish oats, adding orange and dark chocolate for indulgence.

Makes a 23cm (9in) square tin

Base:
175g (6oz) butter
85g (3oz) caster sugar
175g (6oz) self-raising flour
85g (3oz) rolled oats
Grated rind of one large orange

Caramel:
175g (6oz) butter
85g (3oz) granulated or soft brown sugar
400g tin condensed milk
100g (3½ oz) syrup

Topping:
300g (10oz) dark chocolate

Heat the oven to 180°C (160°C fan), 350°F, Gas 4. Oil and line the base of the tin. Cream the butter and sugar. Stir in the remaining ingredients and turn into the tin. Press evenly over the base and bake for 15 minutes until golden and set. Cool.

While the base is baking make the caramel. Put the ingredients into a pan over medium heat and bring to a simmering boil, stirring all the time. Continue to stir until the mixture thickens and turns darker in colour. This takes 5 to 6 minutes. Test by dropping a little caramel into cold water. If it sets to a firm chewy consistency the caramel is ready to pour over the shortbread base. Leave to cool and set, then cover with melted chocolate and cool completely before cutting into squares. Store in an airtight container, up to 1 week.

Baker's note
Cook the caramel on low heat and keep stirring otherwise it may burn. Be patient.

Cakes and Wee Fancies

And now for a 'fancy piece'!

GINGERBREAD

Mummy Clerk's gingerbread

Our next-door neighbour, affectionately known as
Mummy Clerk, made the most delicious baking. Best of
all was her gingerbread.

Makes 2 × 900g (2lb) loaves
15g (½ oz) mixed spice
280g (10oz) self-raising flour
225g (8oz) butter or margarine
225g (8oz) caster or light brown sugar
225g (8oz) golden syrup
3 eggs
Milk, if needed

Heat the oven to 160°C (140°C fan), 325°F, Gas 3. Sift
the flour and spice into a bowl. Cream the butter and
sugar until light. Heat the syrup and add along with the
beaten eggs alternately with a little of the flour to
prevent curdling. Fold in the rest of the flour, adding a
little milk if needed to make a soft dropping consistency.
Bake for 40 minutes then reduce the heat to 150°C
(130°C fan), 300°F, Gas 2 for a further 15 to 20 minutes
or until the cake is risen, firm and the point of a skewer
inserted in the middle comes out cleanly. Cool in the tin.
Wrap in foil and store, up to 10 days. Can be frozen.

Baker's note
Drizzle with lemon water icing for a teatime treat.

Smiddy loaf

An Aberdeenshire farm recipe passed down to my friend Anne by her mother, who was a keen baker. The name 'Smiddy loaf' dates back to when the blacksmith's wife used the forge oven for baking when it had cooled after the smith had finished his day's work.

Makes 1 × 900g (2lb) loaf
115g (4oz) margarine or butter
115g (4oz) caster sugar
225g (8oz) sultanas or mixed fruit
1 cup milk
1 teaspoon mixed spice
1 level teaspoon bicarbonate of soda
2 eggs, beaten
225g (8oz) self-raising flour

Turn on the oven to heat at 160°C (140°C fan) 325°F, Gas 3. Oil and line the loaf tin. Put the margarine, sugar, fruit, milk, spice and bicarbonate of soda into a pan and bring slowly to the boil. Immediately reduce the heat and simmer for 5 minutes. Remove from the heat and cool to blood heat. Add the eggs and sift in the flour. Stir gently together and pour into the prepared tin. Bake a large loaf for 40–45 minutes; the smaller loaves for 30–35 minutes or until the point of a skewer inserted in the middle comes out cleanly. Cool in the tin. Wrap in foil and keep, up to 1 week. Freeze freshly baked.

Janey Buchan's marmalade spice cake

Natives of Moray and family friends Eric and Janey Buchan spent their working lives in Chile but retired back to Elgin. Janey left me her recipe books written in Spanish and English. At the back of one I found this old recipe cut from an Elgin newspaper of the past accompanied with handwritten comments such as 'very good recipe', 'one to keep' and 'make it again'. She must have baked this cake all those thousands of miles away and it is a 'very good recipe'.

Makes a 20cm (8in) round cake

115g (4oz) softened butter
175g (6oz) soft brown sugar
2 eggs
4 tablespoons hot water
300g (10oz) self-raising flour
1 level teaspoon bicarbonate of soda
1 level teaspoon each of ground cinnamon and
    mixed spice
225g (8oz) chunky marmalade

Turn on the oven to heat at 160°C (140°C fan), 325°F, Gas 3. Oil and line a deep 20cm (8 in) round cake tin. Cream the butter and sugar until light, then beat in the eggs one at a time. Stir in the hot water and mix well. Sift the dry ingredients into the mix and fold in carefully, along with the marmalade. Pour into the prepared tin and smooth the top.

Bake for 1 hour in the middle of the oven until risen and firm and the point of a skewer inserted in the middle comes out cleanly. Cool in the tin. Keeps very well and is definitely one to make again!

Baker's note
Make the cake with raspberry or apricot jam instead of marmalade.

Scottish strawberry sponge

A light-as-a-feather sponge to complement fresh Scottish strawberries baked for a birthday surprise. The tasting comment? 'Sooooooooooooooooooo good!'

Makes a cake 20cm (8in) diameter

Sponge:
3 eggs
85g (3oz) caster sugar
115g (4oz) self-raising flour
30g (1oz) melted butter

Filling:
150ml (¼ pint) double cream
A little caster sugar to taste
Vanilla essence
115g (4oz) strawberries, hulled and sliced

Heat the oven to 180°C (160°C fan), 350°F, Gas 4. Oil and line two sandwich tins. Whisk the eggs and sugar until thick and holding the trail of the whisk. If you can, do this over a pan of simmering water because this gently cooks the egg as you whisk. (I find with very fresh eggs this is not necessary.) When the egg is increased in volume, light in colour and holding the trail of the whisk, sift the flour over the mix then fold in very carefully until all the flour is combined, making sure none is stuck to the base of the bowl or the inside of the spoon. Pour the melted butter down the side of the bowl and fold in gently. Divide the mixture between the two tins and bake in the oven for 20 minutes until risen, golden and springy to touch. Cool a little in the tins and then complete cooling on a wire tray.

To make the filling, whip the cream until thick and flavour with a few drops of vanilla essence and a little sugar. Spread the cream on one of the sponges, top with sliced strawberries, then place the second layer of sponge on top. Dust the top of the cake with caster sugar and decorate with a fresh strawberry and a rosette of whipped cream.

Baker's note
You can use any Scottish soft fruit, such as raspberries or blueberries.

Rita's pineapple loaf

A recipe from my friend Rita's family cookery book. Quick, dependable and one I often bake.

Makes 1 × 900g or 2 × 450g (1lb) loaves
115g (4oz) light soft brown sugar
30g (1oz) honey or golden syrup
115g (4oz) butter
Small tin crushed pineapple
350g (12oz) dried fruit – sultanas, currants and raisins
115g (4oz) glacé cherries
2 eggs, beaten
225g (8oz) self-raising flour

Heat the oven to 180°C (160°C fan), 350°F, Gas 4. Oil and line the loaf tins. Melt the sugar and butter, add the pineapple and fruit. Bring to the boil. Cool until just warm then add beaten eggs and flour. Bake the smaller loaves for 30 to 35 minutes and the large loaf for 1 hour or until the point of a skewer inserted in the middle comes out cleanly. Cool in the tins. Wrap in foil and store in an airtight container. This cake keeps well and stays moist for up to two weeks.

Baker's note
Substitute 225g (8oz) of vine fruits with chopped apricots and cranberries.

Madeira cake

Asked to make a Golden Wedding cake, I found a recipe to fit the bill in an old cook book dated 1890, given to me as a gift by Rosemary Merson. It belonged to her late husband Alistair's great aunt, Jessica Munro, who was Andrew Carnegie's housekeeper. I added a lemon curd centre and it worked well.

Makes a 20cm (8in) square cake
280g (10oz) butter
280g (10oz) caster sugar
Grated rind of one large lemon
5 eggs, beaten
280g (10oz) self-raising flour
3 tablespoons lemon curd
Full cream milk to mix

Heat the oven to 180°C (160°C fan), 350°F, Gas 4. Oil and line the cake tin. Cream the butter and sugar until light. Beat in the lemon rind. Gradually beat in the egg alternately with a dessertspoon of flour to prevent curdling. Sift in the rest of the flour and fold in with enough milk (approximately 2 tablespoons) to make a soft dropping consistency.

Spoon half of the mix into the base of the tin and spread evenly. Spread the lemon curd over this and then spoon the rest of the cake mix on top and spread evenly.

Smooth the top using the palm of your hand dipped in a little warm water, then tap the tin sharply on the base. This helps to prevent the cake rising to a peak in the middle as it bakes. Bake for 45 minutes then reduce the temperature to 160°C (140°C fan), 325°F, Gas 3 for a further 15 to 20 minutes. Cool in the tin.

Baker's note
Variations – omit curd and add:

Fruit cake – 225g (8oz) vine fruits and 45g (1½ oz) peel.
Cherry – add 185g (6oz) glacé cherries.
Apple and ginger – add 60g (2oz) chopped apple and 60g (2oz)
    preserved ginger.

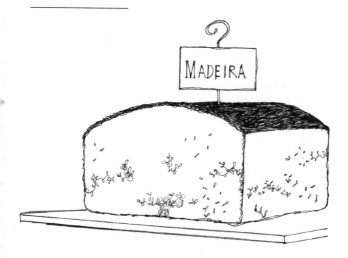

Guinness chocolate cake

My friend Elma Tulloch has a wonderful collection of guild and SWRI recipe books which she kindly lent me on my last visit. This recipe is from one of them.

An indulgent, rich dark chocolate cake for all chocolate lovers to enjoy.

115g (4oz) butter
115g (4oz) soft brown sugar
2 eggs
30g (1oz) cocoa powder
140g (5oz) self raising flour
1 teaspoon baking powder
4 tablespoons Guinness or similar beer

Butter icing:
45g (1½ oz) butter
45g (1½ oz) icing sugar
45g (1½ oz) soft brown sugar
15g (½ oz) cocoa powder
1 or 2 tablespoon Guinness

Topping:
60g (2oz) dark chocolate
30ml (1fl oz) double cream
30g (1oz) soured cream or double cream
30g (1oz) soft brown sugar

Heat the oven to 180°C (160°C fan), 350°F, Gas 4. Oil and line a round baking tin 20cm (8in) or two 18cm (7in) round sandwich tins. Cream the butter and sugar till light, then beat in the eggs. Sift the cocoa, flour and baking powder together and stir into the mix along with the beer. Spread evenly in the prepared tin and bake 25 to 30 minutes for a large cake and 20 to 25 minutes for smaller cakes, till risen and firm. Cool in the tins and place on a wire rack to cool completely.

Make the butter icing by beating the butter and sugars together till light and fluffy, then beat in the cocoa and Guinness. Split the large cake through the middle. Spread the filling between the cakes and sandwich together. Make the topping by melting all the ingredients in a bowl over a water bath and beat smooth. Leave to cool and thicken. Spread over the top of the cake using a flat bladed knife dipped in boiling water. This keeps the shine on the sticky icing.

For gluten free, make sure to use gluten-free beer.

Old-fashioned buns

A selection based on a reliable recipe from the *Dundee Homecraft Book*. Compiled in 1935 by a group of Dundee domestic science teachers, it has educated generations – myself included.

Basic Bun Recipe

Makes 18 to 20 buns
225g (8oz) self-raising flour
1 teaspoon baking powder
85g (3oz) butter or margarine
60g (2oz) sugar
1 egg, beaten
Milk to mix

Now choose which bun you would like to make and follow the recipe below:

Rock – 85g (3oz) currants
Chocolate – 1 tablespoon cocoa powder and a handful of
    chocolate chips
Lemon – grated rind of a small lemon

Heat the oven to 200°C (180°C fan), 400°F, Gas 6. Oil two baking trays. Sift the flour and baking powder into a bowl and rub in the butter. Add your chosen ingredient then mix with beaten egg and enough milk to make a stiff dough. Deposit rough heaps the size of a walnut onto baking trays and bake for 15 minutes until risen and set. Cool on a wire rack.

Raspberry buns
Mix basic bun ingredients to a stiff dough then roll the mixture into balls about the size of a small walnut. Use your thumb to make a hollow in the centre of each and fill with a little raspberry jam. Place on the prepared trays, jam side up, and bake for 15 minutes until golden. Cool a little on the trays and then on a wire rack.

Baker's note
Try a different jam – apricot or blackcurrant works well.

Old men of Hoy

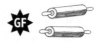

A favourite from the Pomona Café, Kirkwall, Orkney.
These 'peedie' cakes are baked to resemble the famous
Orkney landmark.

Makes 6 to 8 cakes
115g (4oz) softened butter or margarine
115g (4oz) caster sugar
115g (4oz) self-raising flour
1 level teaspoon baking powder
Pinch of salt
2 eggs, beaten

Coating:
4 tablespoons red jam mixed with 1 tablespoon water
60g (oz) desiccated coconut

Topping:
Glacé icing – mix 2 tablespoons icing sugar with a little lemon juice
    until smooth
8 glacé cherries halved

Heat the oven to 180°C (160°C fan), 350°F, Gas 4. Oil
eight mini pudding basins. Cream the butter and sugar.
Sift the flour, baking powder and salt into a bowl.
Gradually beat the eggs into the butter mixture
alternately with a little flour. Fold in the remaining flour
and divide evenly between the moulds filling each about
two-thirds. Smooth the top with the back of a metal

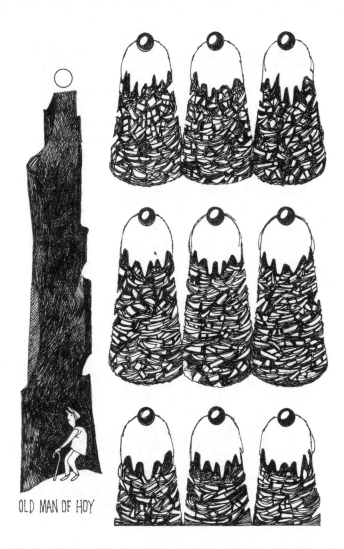

OLD MAN OF HOY

spoon dipped in warm water, making a small dip in the centre to prevent the sponge rising to a peak in the middle. Put the filled moulds on a baking tray and bake in the middle of the oven for 15 to 20 minutes until risen, golden and firm. Cool in the tins on a wire tray. Remove the cakes from the tins and even the base if needed. Lay onto a flat plate. Heat the jam and water in a pan and boil for 1 minute, stirring all the time. Put the coconut on to a sheet of greaseproof paper and make the icing. Make a production line. First brush the sides and narrow top of each cake with jam, roll in the coconut and lay base down on a flat plate. Top with a blob of white icing and place a glacé cherry in the middle. Enjoy freshly baked.

Baker's note
'Peedie' is Orcadian for small or little.

Sair heidies

A recipe from the north east, so named because these small cakes were baked in straight paper cases to represent a bandage, the crushed sugar topping being the aspirins to cure the 'sair heid'!

Makes 6 cakes
60g (2oz) butter or margarine
60g (2oz) caster sugar
2 eggs, beaten
150g (5oz) self-raising flour
Milk to mix
Crushed lump sugar

Heat the oven to 180°C (160°C fan), 350°F, Gas 4. Oil and line 8 muffin tins or, if you have them, metal baking rings approximately 6cm (2½ in) in diameter. Cream the butter and sugar until light then beat in the eggs. Fold in the flour, adding some milk if needed to make a soft dropping consistency. Deposit a dessertspoon of mix into each mould and top with a little crushed sugar. Bake for 15 minutes until risen, set and golden. Cool in the moulds. When cool, remove the rings or paper cases and tie a strip of greaseproof paper round each, securing with string or thread to represent a bandage! An interesting conversation piece!

Wee jam tarts

My mother used leftover pastry to make little jam tarts.
One of the first things my sister and I learned to bake.

Makes 12 tarts

Sweet shortcrust pastry:
225g (8oz) plain flour
115g (4oz) butter
1 dessertspoon caster sugar
1 egg yolk
Cold water

Sift the flour into a bowl and rub in the butter. Mix to a
stiff dough with the egg yolk and water. Knead until
smooth and leave to rest a few minutes.

Try adding a little cinnamon or mixed spice for
festive bakes.

Filling:
Jam, lemon or orange curd or marmalade

Heat the oven to 200°C (180°C fan), 400°F, Gas 6. Oil a
12-hole tart tin. Roll the pastry out on a floured board to
3mm (⅛in) thick. Cut into 12 rounds, making each
round larger than the diameter of each hole to allow
enough pastry to line the base and sides. Drop one or
two teaspoons of filling into each. Roll out the pastry

scraps and cut into small rounds to decorate the middle of each tart. Bake for 15 minutes until the filling is starting to bubble and the pastry is golden. Cool a little in the tin then carefully lift onto a wire cooling rack.

The Hertzoggie – a luxurious jam tart

Recently our new minister, Rev. Attie Van Wyk, arrived from South Africa. As a welcome I baked some 'Hertzoggie', described as a 'confection of buttery pastry filled with apricot jam, topped with coconut meringue'. Named after J.M.B. Hertzog, the former Prime Minister of South Africa. My version went down well and, better still, our new minister recognised my concoction! My baking friends reckon this imported recipe is a winner.

Makes 20 to 24 tarts

Pastry:
25g (8oz) self-raising flour
1 teaspoon baking powder
85g (3oz) caster sugar
Pinch of salt
115g (4oz) cubed soft butter
3 egg yolks
Cold water to mix

Filling:
3 egg whites
115g (4oz) caster sugar
1 teaspoon vanilla essence
115g (4oz) desiccated coconut
Apricot jam or raspberry jam

Heat the oven to 180°C (160°C fan), 350°F, Gas 4. Oil a muffin tin. Sieve the flour, baking powder, salt and caster sugar into a bowl. Rub the butter into the mix until it is like fine breadcrumbs. Add the egg yolks and enough water to make a clean dough. Knead until smooth. Put back into the bowl, cover and rest the dough for 20 minutes. Meanwhile make the meringue. Whisk the egg whites to make soft peaks and slowly add the sugar and vanilla, whisking continuously. Fold in the coconut and set aside. Roll out the pastry on a floured board to 5mm (¼ in) thick. Cut in rounds to line each muffin hollow in the tray. Place a spoon of jam in each and top with meringue. Bake for 20 to 25 minutes until golden. Cool in the tins and remove while warm to a wire rack to cool completely. Store in an airtight container for up to a week, if they last that long!